JBIOG
Presl
Gogerly, Liz

Elvis Presley : the king of rock and roll

Elvis Presley
The King of Rock and Roll

Liz Gogerly

Raintree
Chicago, Illinois

Titles in this series:
Muhammad Ali: The Greatest—Neil Armstrong: The First Man on the Moon—Fidel Castro: Leader of Cuba's Revolution—Roald Dahl: The Storyteller—The Dalai Lama: Peacemaker from Tibet—Anne Frank: Voice of Hope—Mahatma Gandhi: The Peaceful Revolutionary— Bill Gates: Computer Legend—Martin Luther King, Jr.: Civil Rights Hero—John Lennon: Musician with a Message—Nelson Mandela: Father of Freedom—Wolfgang Amadeus Mozart: Musical Genius—Florence Nightingale: The Lady of the Lamp—Pope John Paul II: Pope for the People—Pablo Picasso: Master of Modern Art—Elvis Presley: The King of Rock and Roll—Queen Elizabeth II: Monarch of Our Times—The Queen Mother: Grandmother of a Nation—William Shakespeare: Poet and Playwright—Vincent Van Gogh: The Troubled Artist

© 2004 Raintree
Published by Raintree, a division of Reed Elsevier, Inc.
Chicago, Illinois
Customer Service 888-363-4266
Visit our website at www.raintreelibrary.com

For information, address the publisher:
Raintree, 100 N. LaSalle, Suite 1200, Chicago, IL 60602

Printed in Hong Kong by Wing King Tong.
07 06 05 04 03
10 9 8 7 6 5 4 3 2 1

Library of Congress Cataloging-in-Publication Data:
Gogerly, Liz.
  Elvis Presley / Liz Gogerly.
     p. cm. -- (Famous lives)
Includes index.
Summary: Discusses the life of one of the most famous popular singers of the twentieth century, from his early years in Mississippi to his controversial death at age forty-two.
  ISBN 0-7398-6629-X (lib. bdg.)
  1. Presley, Elvis, 1935-1977--Juvenile literature. 2. Rock musicians--United States--Biography--Juvenile literature. [1. Presley, Elvis, 1935-1977. 2. Singers. 3. Rock music.] I. Title. II. Series: Famous lives (Chicago, Ill.)
  ML3930.P73G64 2004
  782.42166'092--dc21
                     2003005993

Cover: Elvis at the start of his career.
Title page: Elvis performing on stage in the 1950s.

Picture acknowledgments
The publisher would like to thank the following for permission to reproduce photographs:
pp. 4, 12, 13, 19, 21, 32 Corbis; pp. 5, 6, 10, 11, 14, 20, 22, 29, 37, 42 Pictorial Press; pp. 7, 8, 9, 15, 17, 18, 23, 24, 30, 35, 40 Redferns; pp. 16, 34, 43, 44, 45 Topham; pp. 25, 26, 27, 28, 31, 33, 36, 38, 39, 41 Popperfoto.

Cover and title page photos: Pictorial Press

Note to the Reader
Some words are shown in bold, **like this.** You can find out what they mean by looking in the glossary.

Contents

3/2009
Heinemann
$31.43

The King of Rock and Roll   4

Growing up in Mississippi   6

First Guitar   8

The Shy Boy   10

The Lights of Main Street   12

The Big Break   14

Overnight Sensation   16

Storming up the Charts   18

More Smash Hits   20

Lights, Camera, Action!   22

The Big Time   24

Saying Goodbyes   26

A GI in Germany   28

The King is Back!   30

A Life Like the Movies   32

A New Era   34

Behind the Dazzling Smile   36

Las Vegas Elvis   38

Backstage Drama   40

A Fading Star   42

Goodbye to the King   44

Glossary   46

Further Information   46

Date Chart   47

Index   48

The King of Rock and Roll

People tuning in to *The Milton Berle Show* can hardly believe their eyes. It is June 5, 1956, and Elvis Presley is making one of his first television appearances. The 21-year-old ex-truck driver from Tennessee looks wild and dangerous as he sings a **rock-and-roll** song called "Hound Dog." From the tips of his snapping fingers to his shuffling shoes, his body moves to the beat of the music. As he dances and sings, the crowd screams for more.

Elvis performs live in Memphis in July 1956. A few weeks later "Hound Dog" was number one on the U.S. music charts.

Gold records decorate the walls of Elvis's home, Graceland, in Memphis, Tennessee. Elvis earned gold, platinum, and multi-platinum awards for 131 albums and singles in the United States alone.

In the early 1950s, the music **charts** (lists of the most popular records) were dominated by singers that appealed to an older audience. The arrival of Elvis was like an explosion: at last there was somebody whose music spoke to teenagers. Many parents were shocked by Elvis's style of dancing, yet within a year of his appearance on *The Milton Berle Show* he was the top-selling performer of all time. It is estimated that in his lifetime Elvis sold over one billion records worldwide—more than any other musician—but he is most remembered for introducing the world to rock and roll. Although he died in 1977, Elvis Presley is still known as the "King of Rock."

"Elvis Presley ...[,] with his animal gyrations which are certainly most distasteful to me, are violative of [go against] all that I know to be in good taste."
Congressman Emanuel Celler, in *Almost Grown: The Rise of Rock*.

Growing up in Mississippi

Elvis Aaron Presley was born on January 8, 1935, in the town of Tupelo, Mississippi. Elvis's twin brother—Jess Garon—died at birth, and so Vernon and Gladys Presley cherished their surviving child. The 1930s were known as the **Great Depression,** and life in Tupelo was tough. Vernon drifted from one odd job to the next trying to support his family. Then, in 1938, he was jailed for **forging** a check.

Elvis, at about three years old, poses with his parents, Vernon and Gladys.

Times were hard when Elvis was a young boy because his parents did not have much money. To amuse himself, Elvis would make cars out of apple crates or go fishing.

"Don't you worry none.... When I grow up, I'm going to buy you a fine house and pay everything you owe at the grocery store and get two Cadillacs—one for you and Daddy, and one for me."
Gladys Presley remembering what Elvis told her when he was a young boy, in *Last Train to Memphis*.

Vernon was released from prison after eight months, but during this time Gladys could not keep up the payments on the loan for their house and she and Elvis had to live with relatives. Throughout Elvis's childhood, the Presleys moved from one rented place to the next while Vernon tried to make a living. As an adult Elvis rarely spoke about his childhood other than to say it had been hard. Among his best memories were the times he listened to the *Grand Ole Opry*, a live radio show from Nashville, Tennessee, that played country, **gospel,** and **bluegrass** music every Saturday night.

First Guitar

At his first school the teacher described Elvis as "sweet and average." However, it was outside school hours that Elvis showed a flair for music. He longed to sing love songs like the local performer Mississippi Slim, and in 1944 he actually got to sing with his hero on stage. When he was ten he sang in his first talent competition and finished in fifth place. His parents bought him a guitar for his eleventh birthday and he taught himself how to play. On Saturdays he usually went to the weekly **jamboree** held in Tupelo to watch the **bluegrass** entertainers.

The Presleys were religious and regularly attended church. From an early age Elvis sang with his parents in church choirs.

When Elvis started Milam Junior High in 1946, he was considered a lonely misfit. Soon afterward the Presleys moved to a respectable African-American neighborhood in Tupelo. It was an area where many black people lived, at a time when blacks and whites usually lived in different neighborhoods. Now Elvis was listening to the **gospel music** that poured out of the local churches. He also began taking his guitar to school every day, but he was teased about his playing. Some classmates said that he played like a hillbilly, and one time a gang of boys cut the strings of his guitar.

This is the tiny house in Tupolo where Elvis was born and lived until he was thirteen.

The Shy Boy

The blues singer B.B. King at a Memphis radio station in 1950. Elvis often heard him playing live or deejaying on the radio.

In 1948 the Presleys moved to Memphis, Tennessee. Money was so tight that they sometimes ate only corn bread and water. Elvis enrolled at Humes High School, but his close relationship with his mother and his inability to make new friends meant he was teased for being a "mama's boy." Gladys was determined to see her son graduate from high school, however, and in his first year he got an A in language and Bs in history and physical education. Elvis was disappointed that he was given a C for music.

> *"We had to put the lights out before he'd sing.... We had a fire in the fireplace, but it wasn't enough light to show his face. He got way over yonder in the corner—that's just how shy he was."*
> Elvis's Aunt Lillian describing the times when Elvis sang in her living room, in *Last Train to Memphis*.

The city of Memphis was famous for its music, and in the 1940s African-American **blues** singers such as Howlin' Wolf and B.B. King were becoming well known there. By the early 1950s, the blues and African-American **gospel music** were influencing white music, but there were still separate black and white radio stations and record companies. Many whites did not want their children to be influenced by black music. When Elvis tuned in to the local Memphis radio stations he was inspired by all the music he heard, including black music. At night he sat outside his home, quietly strumming his guitar.

Elvis, aged about 15, with his first girlfriend, Betty McMann.

The Lights of Main Street

While he was still in high school, Elvis took odd jobs working in factories or theaters. The extra money meant he could treat himself to a lot of extravagant new clothes. At school, Elvis's unique sense of style really stood out. His hair was different too, because he greased it back with rose oil and Vaseline and grew sideburns. He made a few friends, but he was teased about his new look and banned from the football team because he refused to cut off his **pompadour.**

This early publicity photo shows Elvis at the beginning of his career. He did not start dyeing his naturally light-brown hair black until 1956.

In the 1950s, Beale Street in Memphis was bustling with Cadillacs and filled with shops and clubs where musicians performed. This is how it looks today.

"Here was this classroom full of guys in jeans and T-shirts ... and in the middle sat a dark-haired, dark-eyed boy in a pink sports coat, pink and black pants with ... stripes down each side." George Klein, one of Elvis's school friends from senior year, describing the first time he noticed Elvis, in *Down at the End of Lonely Street: The Life and Death of Elvis Presley.*

Elvis's fascination with music was fueled by his trips to the shops and theaters on Main Street and Beale Street in downtown Memphis. He began hanging out at record shops such as Charlie's and listening to the jukebox. At all-night **gospel** concerts he would marvel at the beauty and power of **spiritual** music. He listened carefully and tried to copy the style at home. At the school talent show in April 1953 he finally made an impression on his classmates. They were moved by the quiet intensity of his voice. Nobody was more surprised than Elvis at how popular he became after that.

The Big Break

In June 1953 Elvis graduated from high school and took a job in a factory. That summer he made a recording of two **ballads** for his mother's birthday at Sam Phillips's Memphis Recording Service. When Phillips heard Elvis sing for the first time, he described his voice as "interesting." One year later, when Phillips needed a vocalist for a new song, he remembered the shy teenager with the promising voice.

Though Elvis never wrote any of the songs he sang, he could play the guitar and piano and enjoyed jamming (improvising).

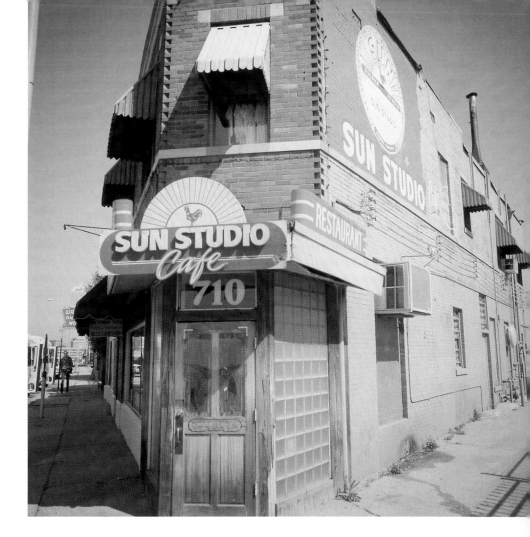

Sun Studio in Memphis is often referred to as the birthplace of rock. Along with Elvis, stars such as Jerry Lee Lewis and Carl Perkins also recorded here.

Elvis was 19, working as a truck driver, and ready to settle down with his girlfriend, Dixie Locke. However, at this next session, Phillips recognized there was something special about Elvis, and in July 1954 Elvis recorded "That's Alright Mama." Phillips got so excited by Elvis's raw vocals and the foot-tapping beat that he asked a local **DJ** named Dewey Phillips to play the record on his show. It had the vitality of African-American music, but it was sung by a white man. Nobody had heard anything like it before. When the song finished playing, the switchboard was jammed with people requesting that he play it again. Within the month, Elvis signed a contract to record music with Sun Records and "That's Alright Mama" was a regional hit.

"Over and over I remember Sam saying, 'If I could find a white man who had the Negro sound and the Negro feel, I could make a billion dollars.' This is what I heard in Elvis." Sam Phillips's secretary Marion Keisker describing the first time she heard Elvis sing, in *Almost Grown: The Rise of Rock.*

Overnight Sensation

On August 10, 1954, Elvis made his first live appearance at Memphis Overton Park. Within months, concerts in his hometown were filled with screaming fans. Newspapers raved about the new musical sensation, describing his sound as a blending of country and African-American **rhythm and blues,** a style of music that was becoming known as **rock and roll.**

Rock and roll was not new. The first white rock and roll group to hit the American pop charts was Bill Haley and the Comets in 1953. Though teenagers loved their sound, Haley did not have the looks or charisma to become the "King of Rock and Roll."

People had not seen anything like Elvis before. Female fans screamed hysterically and men tried to copy him.

Elvis signs autographs for his fans. By 1956 lines of people waited outside his parents' house all day to try to catch a glimpse of him.

"He was a typical teenager. Kind of wild, but ... in a mischievous kind of way. He loved his pranks and practical jokes.... His parents were very protective. His mother would corner me and say 'Take care of my boy. Make sure he eats....'"
Scotty Moore, from Elvis's early band, in *Last Train to Memphis*.

From October 1954 to 1955 Elvis played in towns throughout the American South. He had a special relationship with his fans and always found time to sign autographs. Gladys and Vernon worried about their son's new career. His father did not think there was a future in playing the guitar, and his mother missed him terribly while he was away from home. Elvis's girlfriend, Dixie, hoped that fame would not change him. Nobody guessed just how big Elvis was about to become.

Storming up the Charts

One person who saw the potential in Elvis was a businessman named Colonel Thomas Parker. The Colonel (as Elvis referred to him) became Elvis's manager in mid-1955 and would remain so for the rest of Elvis's life. By this time Elvis had released five **singles,** which had all done well in the South, but the Colonel wanted national stardom. He struck a new deal with the record company RCA, which paid $35,000 for Elvis. At that time this was the highest sum ever paid for a pop star.

Elvis poses with Colonel Tom Parker. The colonel never missed an opportunity to make money from his star.

In January 1956 Elvis released "Heartbreak Hotel." With **blues** piano and a slow electric-guitar solo, it did not have the usual fast-paced **rock and roll** sound. RCA began to panic about their new signing, but in March "Heartbreak Hotel" finally reached the charts. When he sang it live on the Dorsey Brothers *Stage Show* on television, record sales began to rocket. On April 21, "Heartbreak Hotel" jumped to number one on the charts and stayed there for eight weeks.

Elvis performing in the studio in January 1956. By April he was at number one on the U.S. charts.

"The colored folks been singing it and playing it just like I'm doing now, man, for more years than I know.... I got it from them."
Elvis talking about his music in an interview from 1956, in *Last Train to Memphis*.

More Smash Hits

Elvis danced in a new style, swinging his hips in a way that stirred his audiences into a frenzy.

In April 1956 Elvis played live in Las Vegas, the entertainment capital of the United States at the time. Elvis was nervous about playing there, but by now he was a superstar. That year he released **singles** including "Hound Dog," "Blue Suede Shoes," and "Love Me Tender." Fans had never seen or heard anything like him before. His smile melted hearts and his songs touched people's emotions. All his singles stormed to the top of the charts, making Elvis a household name throughout the world. Wherever he went, fans mobbed around him and the media followed him. Even the FBI (Federal Bureau of Investigation) began to monitor his shows because they believed his act was inappropriate. But somehow Elvis remained the same charming country boy he had always been.

"I want the folks back home to think right of me. Just because I managed to do a little something, I don't want anyone back home to think I got a big head."
Elvis in an interview with *Press-Scimitar* in Las Vegas, 1956, in *Last Train to Memphis*.

By the end of 1956 Elvis was feeling the pressure of fame. The support from his fans helped to keep him going.

Fame came at a price. The pressure of touring and promoting his new singles meant he could not spend much time with his new girlfriend, June Juanico. But his biggest problem was lack of sleep. Sometimes he could only grab a few hours' sleep, and often he was plagued by terrible nightmares.

Lights, Camera, Action!

A publicity poster for Elvis's first film, Love Me Tender.

When Elvis stepped in front of television cameras for the first time, his fans were stunned by his brooding good looks. In March 1956 his manager arranged a Hollywood screen test and signed Elvis up for a three-picture deal. In his first role in the film *Love Me Tender,* Elvis played an unlucky cowboy who is killed in a shoot-out. When the film opened in November 1956 it was an immediate hit, and its theme song went to number one on the charts.

"I've made a study of poor Jimmy Dean. I've made a study of myself, and I know why girls, at least the young 'uns, go for us. We're sullen, we're brooding, we're something of a menace." Elvis speaking to a reporter in 1956, in *Almost Grown: The Rise of Rock.*

In 1957 Elvis filmed *Loving You* and *Jailhouse Rock*. As Elvis dazzled his fans with his on-screen presence, the soundtracks from the movies went to the top of the charts. It was a winning combination that propelled Elvis further into the spotlight, and further away from his **rock-and-roll** roots. He spent less time playing live and touring, and more time in Hollywood making films, dating beautiful actresses, and enjoying his newfound wealth. During his lifetime Elvis made 30 films. Among them, his earliest films are widely recognized as his best.

In the film Jailhouse Rock, *from 1957, Elvis played a rock star with a prison background.*

The Big Time

Elvis stands in front of his new home, Graceland. He thought the old-fashioned mansion would make his mother happy.

When Elvis celebrated his twenty-second birthday in 1957 he was already a millionaire, earning more than any other entertainer in the world. Elvis loved to collect cars and motorcycles, and by the end of 1956 he had bought two Harley Davidson motorcycles and three Cadillacs. In March 1957 he finally bought an elegant mansion that matched his superstar status. It was Graceland, located in the outskirts of Memphis. He moved in with his parents, and Elvis insisted that his mother have a beautiful bedroom. He also built her a chicken coop in the garden so she would feel more at home in her grand surroundings.

Elvis appears as a special guest at the launch of the charity "Teens against Polio," held in New York City in January 1957.

"I never expected to be anybody important. Maybe I'm not now, but whatever I am, whatever I will become will be what God has chosen for me.... I just want to let a few people know that the way I live is by doing what I think God wants me to."
Elvis Presley in an interview with *Photoplay* magazine in 1958, in *Last Train to Memphis*.

Despite his luxurious home, Elvis remained fairly unchanged. He still preferred his mother's cooking, especially favorites such as fried chicken and deep-fried banana-and-peanut-butter sandwiches. Never forgetting his humble background, he hosted charity shows to benefit disabled children and other organizations like the Elvis Presley Youth Center in Tupelo.

Saying Goodbyes

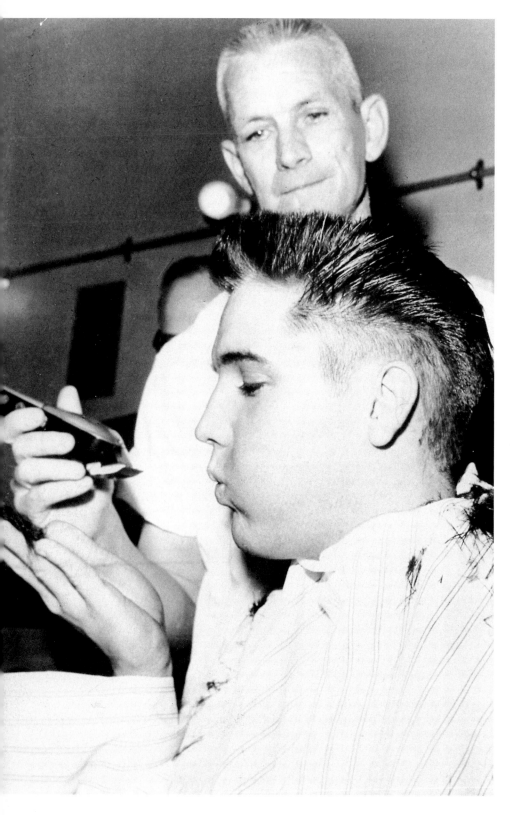

On March 25, 1958, a crowd of photographers and reporters gathered to watch Elvis's famous **pompadour** being shaved off to be replaced with the standard GI (General Infantryman) haircut. Elvis had been called up for two years of service in the military, and he was off to join the army. The millionaire star would now earn less than $100 a month as a soldier. Thousands of fans had written letters to protest his being drafted. Elvis was not pleased about joining the army, either, but he recognized it was his duty. By the summer of 1958, Private Presley was posted at Fort Hood in Texas to complete his army training.

Elvis looks a little nervous as his hair is cut into the traditional GI buzz cut.

Although he lived outside of the military base with his parents, he worked hard to prepare for his overseas assignment in Germany. In private he felt homesick and worried that his fans would forget him while he was away. He feared it would be the end of his musical career. It seemed that things could not get any worse, but then in August, his mother died from liver disease. At her funeral Elvis nearly collapsed with grief. People thought he looked sad and lost when he boarded the train on his way to Germany that September.

"Mother was always right with me all my life. And it wasn't only like losing a mother, it was like losing a friend, a companion, someone to talk to...."
Elvis talking about the loss of his mother in a press conference before he left for Germany, in *Last Train to Memphis*.

Elvis kisses his beloved mother goodbye when he joins the U.S. Army in March 1958.

A GI in Germany

Even famous stars have to clean their own boots in the army. Elvis looks tired and sad in this photograph taken in Germany in November 1958.

Elvis wanted to be just like the other soldiers. While he was stationed in Germany he refused to make records for RCA and turned down all requests to entertain the troops. However, when he was greeted in Germany by 1,500 fans, it was obvious that life in the army would never be regular for Private Presley. Within days his request to live off base with his father and his grandmother, who had also moved to Germany, was accepted, and he was given a driver to help keep him out of the public eye.

Elvis had many girlfriends while he was in Germany, but Priscilla was special.

Despite his special treatment, Elvis was a good soldier who was popular around the base. Despite having early-morning duties like the other soldiers, he still hosted late-night parties at his home in the German town of Bad Nauheim. At these parties he would sing his favorite **gospel music** for his friends. It was during one of these parties that he met Priscilla Beaulieu, the daughter of an army captain. Although she was younger than he was, Elvis liked her at once and began to spend time with her. Priscilla eventually would become an important part of Elvis's life.

The King is Back!

In March 1960 Elvis said goodbye to Priscilla and army life and returned home to Graceland. Two years before, Elvis had sold a record-breaking eighteen million **singles**— to date no other artist has beaten that record. That May, when his new single "Stuck on You" was a hit, it seemed he still had that old magic. The next test came when he appeared on *The Frank Sinatra Show,* in a special called *Welcome Home, Elvis.* Years earlier Sinatra, nicknamed "The King of Crooners," had called Elvis's music "deplorable." The meeting of the two "kings" could have been a disaster, but Elvis proved he could still compete with the best entertainers in the world.

Elvis and Sinatra sang together on the **Welcome Home, Elvis** *show. When it was shown in May 1960, nearly 68 percent of television viewers in the United States tuned in.*

That year Elvis had number-one hits with the old-fashioned **ballad** "Are You Lonesome Tonight?" and the love song "It's Now or Never." Most fans remained loyal to Elvis, but some began to wonder if the army had tamed him completely—his music did not seem to be as wild and gutsy as it had before. When Elvis returned to Hollywood to make films like *GI Blues* and *Flaming Star,* it looked like he had turned his back on **rock and roll** for good.

Elvis on the set of GI Blues in July 1960. In this musical comedy, Elvis plays a soldier posted in Germany.

A Life Like the Movies

In March 1961 Elvis performed a live concert in Honolulu, Hawaii. The crowd went crazy as Elvis delivered one of the best performances of his life. Unfortunately for his fans, they would not see him perform live again for nearly eight years. Elvis focused on his growing film career, starring in *Blue Hawaii* and *Viva Las Vegas* with gorgeous leading ladies in exotic locations. Sadly, the plots had become too predictable and Elvis began to resent the deals made by the Colonel that kept him tied to Hollywood.

In the musical comedy **Blue Hawaii (1962),** *Elvis leaves the army and takes a job with a Hawaiian tourist agency. Life is rosy until too much attention from a group of schoolgirls threatens his relationship with his girlfriend.*

When Elvis finally married Priscilla in 1967, it looked like a real-life fairy tale.

"I ... became very interested [in] reading about religions. I was interested in self-realization—in finding one's true self. Who isn't? [But] I have never left my own church."
Elvis explaining his search for spirituality to May Mann, a Hollywood gossip columnist, in *Careless Love: The Unmaking of Elvis Presley*.

As he grew older, he became more **spiritual** as he searched for answers about his own life. In other ways, though, he became wilder. He surrounded himself with a gang of friends, who became known as "the Memphis Mafia" and acted as his bodyguards. They hosted all-night parties and Elvis had many different girlfriends. Meanwhile, Priscilla Beaulieu waited patiently for Elvis to marry her. They were eventually married in 1967, and nine months later they had a daughter whom they named Lisa Marie.

A New Era

In 1964 a new band from England called The Beatles was creating the kind of sensation that Elvis had caused in 1956. The Beatles had been inspired by Elvis, but when they met him in August 1965 they were disappointed. They found that they did not have much in common. One of the Beatles, John Lennon, even asked Elvis when he would get back to playing genuine **rock and roll.** Elvis became more determined to perform concerts and to record music with more meaning.

In 1964 The Beatles had their first number-one song in the United States. They were influenced by Elvis's music.

"I will never sing a song I don't believe in again. I will never make another movie I don't believe in again."
Elvis in 1968 following the success of his television special, in *Down at the End of Lonely Street.*

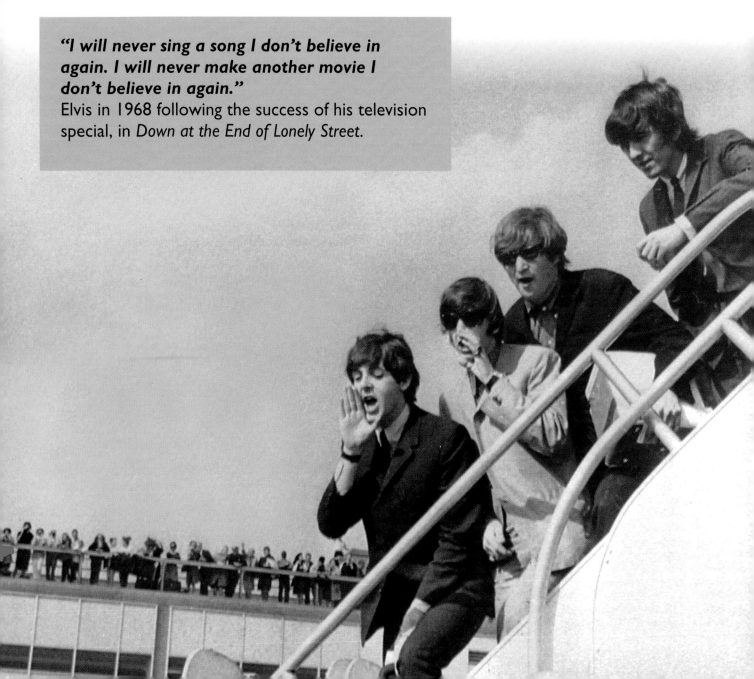

Wearing a stylish black leather outfit, Elvis made his comeback on a television special in 1968.

It was not until 1968 that Elvis finally performed live again. At the end of the show, he sang "If I Can Dream." It was the first time that Elvis had sung a song that addressed the current situation in the United States. It was the year that African-American leader Martin Luther King Jr. and presidential candidate Robert F. Kennedy had both been assassinated, and American troops were fighting in Vietnam. The following year he released "In the **Ghetto**," a moving song about poverty in the black ghettos of U.S. cities. Later that year, when the emotional "Suspicious Minds" went to number one, it seemed as if Elvis's magic touch had been restored.

Behind the Dazzling Smile

Many people believed that Elvis's comeback was partly due to the happiness he had found as a family man. They thought his marriage to Priscilla was like a fairy tale, but in truth Elvis's marriage was not working out very well. He preferred the company of the Memphis Mafia and did not spend very much time at home. Elvis had also become more dependent on **prescription drugs,** which brought on mood swings and panic attacks.

"During the lulls he wouldn't know what to do with himself. He was like a child. He would take pills or read or just eat— because he was bored. You know, he just had to occupy his time with something to do." Priscilla Presley, in *Careless Love: The Unmaking of Elvis Presley.*

Elvis with Priscilla and a newborn Lisa Marie in February 1968. Elvis called Lisa Marie "a little miracle."

To the world Elvis appeared to be a larger-than-life character who had everything a man could want. Behind the scenes, though, Elvis was searching for the security and happiness that had been absent from his life since his mother's death. When he was not out all night with the Memphis Mafia, he stayed up all night in his bedroom watching television, reading **spiritual** books, and eating junk food. He also spent millions of dollars on diamond jewelry or cars and houses for his friends. The only time he felt any real joy was when he was performing for his fans.

This family photograph was taken in February 1971. Although they appear happy, there were many problems with Elvis and Priscilla's marriage.

Las Vegas Elvis

Elvis charms journalists at a press conference at the International Hotel in Las Vegas in July 1969.

When Elvis played Las Vegas in the 1950s he had felt out of touch with the older audience. In July 1969 he was 34 and ready to take Vegas by storm. On the stage at the International Hotel, the gold curtains went up to reveal Elvis dressed in colorful clothes and accompanied by a full orchestra and backup singers. He performed many of his old hits but his voice was more expressive. He added new dance steps, including karate kicks and cartwheels. He laughed and joked with the audience as he told them about his life. He was a natural entertainer, and was rewarded with cheers and **standing ovations.**

Between 1969 and 1977, Elvis performed over 1,000 shows. Many of these were in Las Vegas, where his shows were always sold out. As the years went by, his costumes became more elaborate. He became famous for his all-white jumpsuits studded with artifical jewels, and large belt buckles. Along with his old songs, he introduced new **ballads** and **gospel music.** Even when he became overweight and his looks began to fade, his fans always screamed for more.

"But as the years went by it got harder and harder to perform to a movie camera, and I really missed the people, I really missed contact with a live audience. And I just wanted to tell you how good it is to be back."
Elvis speaking to his audience during one of his Las Vegas shows in 1969, in *Careless Love: The Unmaking of Elvis Presley.*

Elvis appears every bit the star in this early photograph from the Las Vegas years.

Backstage Drama

In 1970, during what was advertised as Elvis's "comeback tour," he was thrilled to be playing live again and mixing with other celebrities. The satisfaction was short-lived, though, and he soon became bored. Part of his frustration was his manager's refusal to allow a world tour. Elvis also became very worried about his own safety, and spent large amounts of money on guns.

Elvis's stage act and outfits became more and more outrageous. He was known for wearing pants with flared legs and plenty of chunky jewelry.

Elvis shakes hands with President Nixon in December 1970. He offered to help the president fight against the rise in illegal drug use, in spite of his own addictions.

"I talked to Vice President Agnew in Palm Springs three weeks ago and expressed my concern for our country. Sir I can and will be of any service that I can to help the country out...."
Taken from Elvis's letter to President Nixon, December 1970, in *Careless Love: The Unmaking of Elvis Presley.*

On December 19, 1970, Priscilla and Elvis's father, Vernon, tried to tell him that his expensive lifestyle was going to bankrupt him. He flew into a rage and walked out on them. It was a mystery where he had gone, but two days later Elvis made an unannounced visit to President Richard M. Nixon at the White House in Washington, D.C. The King of **Rock and Roll**, who was hooked on **prescription drugs** himself, offered the president his support in the fight against illegal drugs. Elvis's offer of help was sincere, but it showed how confused he was becoming.

A Fading Star

This photograph of Elvis was taken in June 1972.

In December 1971 Priscilla finally left Elvis and took Lisa Marie with her. Even though he had not been happy with their marriage, Elvis was angry and depressed. When he released "Always on My Mind" in November 1972 it was as if he was pouring his heart into the song. His voice sounded hurt and full of regrets.

A rich lifestyle did not fill the emptiness in Elvis's life. A high point was a charity show in Hawaii in January 1973. The show was broadcast by satellite around the world to an estimated audience of one billion. Elvis appeared slim and healthy, but within months he became bloated and ill. That year doctors pulled Elvis back from the brink of death four times after he overdosed on **prescription drugs.** By 1975 Elvis was making fewer live appearances, and when he did he was often dazed and forgot the words to his songs. Many people said his voice was better than ever, but Elvis was on his way out of the spotlight.

"*The Living Legend was fat and ludicrously aping [imitating] his former self.... His personality was lost in one of the most ill-prepared, unsteady, and most disheartening performances of his Las Vegas career.*"
From a concert review in the *Hollywood Reporter* in 1973, in *Elvis Day By Day*.

Elvis shows off one of his typical stage costumes as he performs later in his life.

Goodbye to the King

Elvis played his final show on June 26, 1977, in Indianapolis, Indiana. He planned to tour again, but on August 16 he was found dead in his bathroom at Graceland. Elvis was just 42 years old, but he died of a heart attack, brought on by years of drug abuse and overeating. When the news broke later that day, huge crowds gathered outside Graceland to pay their final respects. All over the world, shocked fans tried to come to terms with the death of the King of **Rock and Roll.**

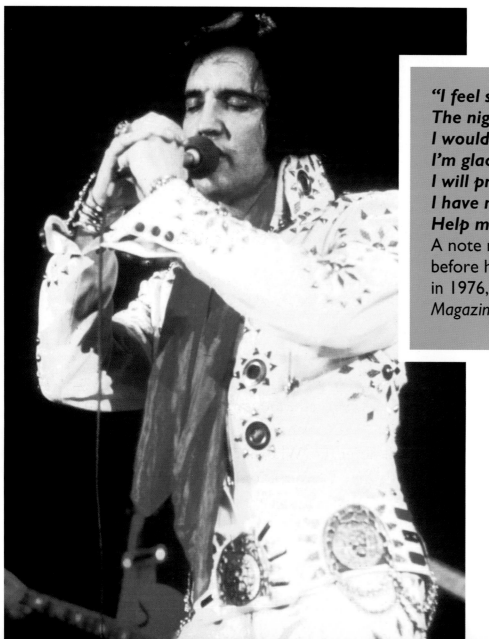

"I feel so alone sometimes
The night is quiet for me
I would love to be able to sleep
I'm glad everyone is gone now
I will probably not rest tonight
I have no need for all of this
Help me Lord"
A note made by Elvis a few days before his final Las Vegas show in 1976, in *Mojo: The Music Magazine*, April 2002.

In June 1977—around the same time as the performance in this picture—Elvis released "Way Down," the last single to be released during his lifetime.

The final resting place of Elvis Presley on the grounds of Graceland. Tours of Graceland, which began in 1982, include a few quiet moments at the graveside of the "King."

Today, Elvis's resting place is next to his mother in the Meditation Garden behind Graceland. Each August on the anniversary of his death, thousands of fans still make a **pilgrimage** to Graceland. Many Elvis fans claim that the "King" will never die. When a **remixed** version of the 1968 hit "A Little Less Conversation" was released in the summer of 2002, it seemed they were proved right. Once more Elvis went to the top of the charts, and a whole new generation was introduced to his music.

Glossary

ballad slow, sentimental song

bluegrass country music usually played on mandolins, banjos, and guitars

blues sad music first sung by African Americans in the early 20th century

chart list of most popular songs or albums

DJ (also spelled *deejay*) disc jockey; person who plays music on a radio show

forging to sign someone else's name on a document, usually to steal their money

ghetto poor residential area

Great Depression period of hard economic times in the United States, between 1929 and around 1940

gospel music style of religious music that developed from the songs sung in African-American churches

gyration circular movement

jamboree large celebration

pilgrimage journey to a place that holds great emotional or spiritual meaning

pompadour hairstyle in which hair is combed into a tuft above the forehead

prescription drugs drugs that are given to an individual by a doctor

remixed when an old song is made into a new version, using parts of the original recording but usually set to a new beat

rhythm and blues music that includes elements of blues and jazz

rock and roll music with a strong beat that became popular in the 1950s

single song that is released to radio stations to be played on the air

spiritual having to do with religious beliefs; also a religious song

standing ovation when an audience stands up and applauds a performer

Further Information

Books to Read:

Denenberg, Barry. *All Shook Up: The Life and Death of Elvis Presley.* New York: Scholastic, 2001.

Matthews, Rupert. *Profiles: Elvis Presley.* Chicago: Heinemann, 2001.

Sources of Quotes:

Brown, Peter, and Pat Broeske. *Down at the End of Lonely Street: The Life and Death of Elvis Presley.* New York: Arrow Books, 1998.

Guralnick, Peter. *Careless Love: The Unmaking of Elvis Presley.* New York: Little, Brown, 1999.

Guralnick, Peter. *Last Train to Memphis: The Rise of Elvis Presley.* New York: Little, Brown, 1994.

Guralnic, Peter, and Ernst Jorgensen.*Elvis Day by Day: The Definitive Record of his Life and Music.* New York: Ballantine, 1999.

Miller, James. *Almost Grown: The Rise of Rock.* London: William Heinemann, 1999.

Date Chart

January 8, 1935 Elvis Aaron Presley born in Tupelo, Mississippi.

1948 Moves to Memphis, Tennessee with his family.

1954 Records "That's Alright Mama" and "Blue Moon of Kentucky" at Memphis Recording Service. He plays live at Overton Park and signs a contract with Sun Records.

1955 Colonel Thomas Parker becomes Elvis's manager. Elvis signs a contract with RCA records.

1956 Elvis appears on television for the first time. "Heartbreak Hotel" reaches number one on the U.S. charts and becomes his first release in Great Britain. Elvis releases "Don't Be Cruel," "Hound Dog," "Blue Suede Shoes," and "Love Me Tender." He stars in his first movie, *Love Me Tender*.

1957 Releases "All Shook Up" and "Jailhouse Rock." He buys Graceland in Memphis.

1958 Drafted into the army. Gladys Presley dies of liver failure shortly before Elvis leaves for his military assignment in Germany.

1959 Meets Priscilla Beaulieu in Bad Nauheim, German.

1960 Returns to the United States. He releases the singles "Stuck on You" and "Are You Lonesome Tonight?" He stars in the movie *GI Blues*, and appears on *The Frank Sinatra Show* special, *Welcome Home, Elvis,* where he sings a duet with Sinatra.

1965 The Beatles visit Elvis at his home in Hollywood.

1967 Elvis marries Priscilla Beaulieu in Las Vegas, Nevada.

1968 Elvis's daughter, Lisa Marie Presley, is born. He releases "If I Can Dream," which he sings on a television special watched by 42 percent of the U.S. viewing audience.

1969 Releases "In the Ghetto" and "Suspicious Minds." He opens a month-long engagement in Las Vegas at the International Hotel.

1970 Meets President Richard M. Nixon in the White House.

1977 Plays final live show at Market Square Arena, Indianapolis, Indiana. His last single, "Way Down," is released. On **August 16,** Elvis dies at Graceland. Following attempts to steal his body, Elvis's remains are moved to the Meditation Garden behind Graceland and laid to rest next to his mother. "Way Down" reaches number one in the months after his death.

2002 "A Little Less Conversation," the first remix of an Elvis song, reaches number one in the United States and Great Britain and tops the charts in countries all over the world.

Index

All numbers in **bold** refer to pictures as well as text.

"Always on My Mind" 42

"Are You Lonesome
   Tonight?" 31

Beatles, The **34**, 41
Beaulieu, Priscilla *see* Presley,
   Priscilla
black music 9, 11, 19
"Blue Suede Shoes" 20

Dean, James 22
drug abuse 29, 36, 42, 44

FBI 20
films **22–23**, **31**, **32**, 34
food 10, 25

Germany 28–29
gospel music 7, 9, 11, 13, 29,
   38
Graceland 5, **24**, 44, **45**
Grand Ole Opry 7

Haley, Bill 16
Hawaii 32, 42
"Heartbreak Hotel" 19
"Hound Dog" 4, 20
Howlin' Wolf 11

"If I Can Dream" 35
"In the Ghetto" 35
"It's Now or Never" 31

Kennedy, Robert F. 35
King, B.B. **10**, 11
King Jr., Martin Luther 35

Las Vegas 20, 38, 43
Lennon, John **34**
Lewis, Jerry Lee 15
"Little Less Conversation, A"
   45
"Love Me Tender" 20, 22

McCartney, Paul **34**
Memphis Mafia 33, 36
Mississippi Slim 8

national service 26–29
Nixon, Richard M. **41**

Parker, Colonel Tom **18**, 22,
   32, 40
Perkins, Carl 15
Phillips, Sam 14, 15
Presley, Elvis Aaron
   birth 6
   clothes 12, 13, 38, **40**
   hairstyle **12**, **26**
   death 44
   drug abuse 36, 42, 41, 44
   marriage **33**, **36**, 37, 42
   national service 26–29
   school 8, 9, 10, 13, 14
   spirituality 25, 33, 37

weight problems 38, 42,
   43
Presley, Gladys (mother) **6**,
   7, **8**, 10, 17, **27**
   death 27, 37
Presley, Lisa Marie (daughter)
   33, **36**, **37**, 42
Presley, Priscilla (wife) **29**,
   30, **33**, **36**, **37**, 41, 42
Presley, Vernon (father) **6**, 7,
   8, 17, **27**, 41, 45

RCA 18, 19, 28
recordings 5, 14, 15, 19, 20,
   30, 31, 34, 35, 42, 44, 45
rock and roll 5, 15, 16, 31,
   34, 41, 44

Sinatra, Frank **30**
spirituality 25, 33, 37, 44
"Stuck on You" 30
Sun Records 15
Sun Studio **15**
"Suspicious Minds" 35

television appearances 4, 19,
   22, **30**, 34, **35,** 42
"That's Alright Mama" 15
Tupelo 6, 8, 9

"Way Down" 44